A CHILD'S
GARDEN *of* VERSES

ROBERT LOUIS STEVENSON

Illustrated by Eric Kincaid

This edition published in the UK by Brimax Publishing Ltd
Appledram Barns, Chichester, PO20 7EQ, UK

First published by Brimax Books Ltd, 1996
This format first published by
The Five Mile Press Pty Ltd, 2006

Illustrations copyright © Eric Kincaid, 1996
This format copyright © The Five Mile Press Pty Ltd, 2006
CD produced by Spoken Word Productions

CONTENTS

$\mathscr{I}$NTRODUCTION

Robert Louis Stevenson was well-known in the literary circles of his day as a novelist, essayist and poet. He is now chiefly remembered for the adventure stories he wrote for children, *Treasure Island*, and *Kidnapped*, and for the book of verse he wrote about his childhood, *A Child's Garden of Verses*.

Stevenson was born in Edinburgh in 1850 and his childhood was active and happy in spite of much illness caused by a weakness of the lungs. Little of such childhood illness is reflected by the cheerfulness of *A Child's Garden of Verses*. Stevenson spent much of his adult life travelling the world, seeking healthier climates than that of his native Scotland. So it is not surprising to discover *A Child's Garden of Verses* was written over a number of years in three different countries. It was begun in Braemar in Scotland, in the summer of 1881. *Treasure Island* then took precedence and it was not until 1883, whilst convalescing in the South of France, that Stevenson wrote more poems. His collection of verses was completed in Bournemouth, England, in 1884.

A small volume of plainly printed poems was finally published in 1885; it had an immediate and enduring success. It has been suggested that Stevenson was inspired by Kate Greenaway's *Birthday Book for Children* published in 1880. But it was not until 1895, a year after Stevenson's death in Samoa, that the first illustrated version of *A Child's Garden of Verses* by Charles Robinson appeared.

This abridged edition of the book is illustrated by Eric Kincaid, who brings a fresh charm to these eternal verses for another generation of children.

DEDICATION

TO ALISON CUNNINGHAM FROM HER BOY

For the long nights you lay awake
And watched for my unworthy sake:
For your most comfortable hand
That led me through the uneven land:
For all the story-books you read,
For all the pains you comforted,
For all you pitied, all you bore,
In sad and happy days of yore: –
My second Mother, my first Wife,
The angel of my infant life –
From the sick child, now well and old,
Take, nurse, the little book you hold!

And grant it, Heaven, that all who read
May find as dear a nurse at need,
And every child who lists my rhyme,
In the bright fireside, nursery clime,
May hear it in as kind a voice
As made my childish days rejoice!

R.L.S.

RAIN

The rain is raining all around,
It falls on field and tree,
It rains on the umbrellas here,
And on the ships at sea.

NEST EGGS

Birds all the sunny day
  Flutter and quarrel
Here in the arbour-like
  Tent of the laurel.

Here in the fork
  The brown nest is seated;
Four little blue eggs
  The mother keeps heated.

While we stand watching her,
  Staring like gabies,
Safe in each egg are the
  Bird's little babies.

Soon the frail eggs they shall
  Chip, and upspringing
Make all the April woods
  Merry with singing.

Younger than we are,
  O children, and frailer,
Soon in blue air they'll be
  Singer and sailor.

We, so much older,
  Taller and stronger,
We shall look down on the
  Birdies no longer.

They shall go flying
  With musical speeches
High overhead in the
  Tops of the beeches.

In spite of our wisdom
  And sensible talking,
We on our feet must go
  Plodding and walking.

THE FLOWERS

All the names I know from nurse:
Gardener's garters, Shepherd's purse,
Bachelor's buttons, Lady's smock,
And the Lady Hollyhock.

Fairy places, fairy things,
Fairy woods where the wild bee wings,
Tiny trees for tiny dames –
These must all be fairy names!

Tiny woods below whose boughs
Shady fairies weave a house;
Tiny tree-tops, rose or thyme,
Where the braver fairies climb!

Fair are grown-up people's trees,
But the fairest woods are these;
Where if I were not so tall,
I should live for good and all.

A GOOD PLAY

We built a ship upon the stairs
All made of the back-bedroom chairs,
And filled it full of sofa pillows
To go a-sailing on the billows.

We took a saw and several nails,
And water in the nursery pails;
And Tom said, 'Let us also take
An apple and a slice of cake';
Which was enough for Tom and me
To go a-sailing on, till tea.

We sailed along for days and days,
And had the very best of plays;
But Tom fell out and hurt his knee,
So there was no one left but me.

WHERE GO THE BOATS?

Dark brown is the river,
  Golden is the sand.
It flows along for ever,
  With trees on either hand.

Green leaves a-floating,
  Castles of the foam,
Boats of mine a-boating –
  Where will all come home?

On goes the river
  And out past the mill,
Away down the valley,
  Away down the hill.

Away down the river,
  A hundred miles or more,
Other little children
  Shall bring my boats ashore.

MARCHING SONG

Bring the comb and play upon it!
  Marching, here we come!
Willie cocks his highland bonnet,
  Johnnie beats the drum.

Mary Jane commands the party,
  Peter leads the rear;
Feet in time, alert and hearty,
  Each a Grenadier!

All in the most martial manner
  Marching double-quick;
While the napkin like a banner
  Waves upon the stick!

LOOKING FORWARD

When I am grown to man's estate
I shall be very proud and great,
And tell the other girls and boys
Not to meddle with my toys.

THE COW

The friendly cow, all red and white,
  I love with all my heart:
She gives me cream with all her might,
  To eat with apple-tart.

She wanders lowing here and there,
  And yet she cannot stray,
All in the pleasant open air,
  The pleasant light of day;

And blown by all the winds that pass
  And wet with all the showers,
She walks among the meadow grass
  And eats the meadow flowers.

HAPPY THOUGHT

The world is so full
of a number of things,
I'm sure we should all
be as happy as kings.

THE WIND

I saw you toss the kites on high
And blow the birds about the sky;
And all around I heard you pass,
Like ladies' skirts across the grass –
  O wind, a-blowing all day long,
  O wind, that sings so loud a song!

I saw the different things you did,
But always you yourself you hid.
I felt you push, I heard you call,
I could not see yourself at all –
  O wind, a-blowing all day long,
  O wind, that sings so loud a song!

O you that are so strong and cold,
O blower, are you young or old?
Are you a beast of field and tree,
Or just a stronger child than me?
  O wind, a-blowing all day long,
  O wind, that sings so loud a song!

KEEPSAKE MILL

Over the borders, a sin without pardon,
  Breaking the branches and crawling below,
Out through the breach in the wall of the garden,
  Down by the banks of the river, we go.

Here is the mill with the humming of thunder,
  Here is the weir with the wonder of foam,
Here is the sluice with the race running under –
  Marvellous places, though handy to home!

Sounds of the village grow stiller and stiller,
  Stiller the note of the birds on the hill;
Dusty and dim are the eyes of the miller,
  Deaf are his ears with the moil of the mill.

Years may go by, and the wheel in the river
  Wheels as it wheels for us, children, to-day,
Wheel and keep roaring and foaming for ever
  Long after all of the boys are away.

Home from the Indies, and home from the ocean,
  Heroes and soldiers we all shall come home;
Still we shall find the old mill-wheel in motion,
  Turning and churning that river to foam.

You with the bean that I gave when we quarrelled,
  I with your marble of Saturday last,
Honoured and old and all gaily apparelled,
  Here we shall meet and remember the past.

AUNTIE'S SKIRT

Whenever Auntie moves around,
Her dresses make a curious sound;
They trail behind her up the floor,
And trundle after through the door.

THE LAND OF COUNTERPANE

When I was sick and lay a-bed,
I had two pillows at my head,
And all my toys beside me lay
To keep me happy all the day.

And sometimes for an hour or so
I watched my leaden soldiers go,
With different uniforms and drills,
Among the bed-clothes, through the hills;

And sometimes sent my ships in fleets
All up and down among the sheets;
Or brought my trees and houses out,
And planted cities all about.

I was the giant great and still
That sits upon the pillow-hill,
And sees before him, dale and plain,
The pleasant land of counterpane.

GOOD AND BAD CHILDREN

Children, you are very little,
And your bones are very brittle;
If you would grow great and stately,
You must try to walk sedately.

You must still be bright and quiet,
And content with simple diet;
And remain, through all bewild'ring,
Innocent and honest children.

Happy hearts and happy faces,
Happy play in grassy places –
That was how, in ancient ages,
Children grew to kings and sages.

But the unkind and the unruly,
And the sort to eat unduly,
They must never hope for glory –
Theirs is quite a different story!

Cruel children, crying babies,
All grow up as geese and gabies,
Hated, as their age increases,
By their nephews and their nieces.

THE LAND OF NOD

From breakfast on all through the day
At home among my friends I stay;
But every night I go abroad
Afar into the Land of Nod.

All by myself I have to go,
With none to tell me what to do –
All alone beside the streams
And up the mountain-sides of dreams.

The strangest things are there for me,
Both things to eat and things to see,
And many frightening sights abroad
Till morning in the Land of Nod.

Try as I like to find the way,
I never can get back by day,
Nor can remember plain and clear
The curious music that I hear.

MY SHADOW

I have a little shadow that goes in and out with me,
And what can be the use of him is more than I can see.
He is very, very like me from the heels up to the head;
And I see him jump before me, when I jump into my bed.

The funniest thing about him is the way he likes to grow –
Not at all like proper children, which is always very slow;
For he sometimes shoots up taller like an india-rubber ball,
And he sometimes gets so little that there's none of him at all.

He hasn't got a notion of how children ought to play,
And can only make a fool of me in every sort of way.
He stays so close behind me he's a coward you can see;
I'd think shame to stick to nursie as that shadow sticks to me!

One morning, very early, before the sun was up,
I rose and found the shining dew on every buttercup;
But my lazy little shadow, like an arrant sleepy-head,
Had stayed at home behind me and was fast asleep in bed.

THE SUN'S TRAVELS

The sun is not a-bed when I
At night upon my pillow lie;
Still round the earth his way he takes,
And morning after morning makes.

While here at home, in shining day,
We round the sunny garden play,
Each little Indian sleepy-head
Is being kissed and put to bed.

And when at eve I rise from tea,
Day dawns beyond the Atlantic Sea,
And all the children in the West
Are getting up and being dressed.

THE LAMPLIGHTER

My tea is nearly ready
   and the sun has left the sky;
It's time to take the window
   to see Leerie going by;
For every night at tea-time
   and before you take your seat,
With lantern and with ladder
   he comes posting up the street.

Now Tom would be a driver
   and Maria go to sea,
And my papa's a banker
   and as rich as he can be;
But I, when I am stronger
   and can choose what I'm to do,
O Leerie, I'll go round at night
   and light the lamps with you!

For we are very lucky,
   with a lamp before the door,
And Leerie stops to light it
   as he lights so many more;
And O! before you hurry by
   with ladder and with light,
O Leerie, see a little child
   and nod to him to-night!

THE MOON

The moon has a face like the clock in the hall;
She shines on thieves on the garden wall,
On streets and fields and harbour quays,
And birdies asleep in the forks of the trees.

The squalling cat and the squeaking mouse,
The howling dog by the door of the house,
The bat that lies in bed at noon,
All love to be out by the light of the moon.

But all of the things that belong to the day
Cuddle to sleep to be out of her way;
And flowers and children close their eyes
Till up in the morning the sun shall rise.

LOOKING-GLASS RIVER

Smooth it slides upon its travel,
 Here a wimple, there a gleam –
  O the clean gravel!
  O the smooth stream!

Sailing blossoms, silver fishes,
 Paven pools as clear as air –
  How a child wishes
  To live down there!

We can see our coloured faces
 Floating on the shaken pool
  Down in cool places,
  Dim and very cool;

Till a wind or water wrinkle,
  Dipping marten, plumping trout,
    Spreads in a twinkle
    And blots all out.

See the rings pursue each other;
  All below grows black as night,
    Just as if mother
    Had blown out the light!

Patience, children, just a minute –
  See the spreading circles die;
    The stream and all in it
    Will clear by-and-by.

THE HAYLOFT

Through all the pleasant meadow-side
  The grass grew shoulder-high,
Till the shining scythes went far and wide
  And cut it down to dry.

These green and sweetly smelling drops
  They led in wagons home;
And they piled them here in mountain tops
  For mountaineers to roam.

Here is Mount Clear, Mount Rusty-Nail,
  Mount Eagle and Mount High; –
The mice that in these mountains dwell,
  No happier are than I!

O what a joy to clamber there,
  O what a place for play,
With the sweet, the dim, the dusty air,
  The happy hills of hay.

FAREWELL TO THE FARM

The coach is at the door at last;
The eager children, mounting fast
And kissing hands, in chorus sing:
Good-bye, good-bye, to everything!

To house and garden, field and lawn,
The meadow-gates we swang upon,
To pump and stable, tree and swing,
Good-bye, good-bye, to everything!

And fare you well for evermore,
O ladder at the hayloft door,
O hayloft where the cobwebs cling,
Good-bye, good-bye, to everything!

Crack goes the whip, and off we go;
The trees and houses smaller grow;
Last, round the woody turn we swing:
Good-bye, good-bye, to everything!

TRAVEL

I should like to rise and go
Where the golden apples grow;
Where below another sky
Parrot islands anchored lie,
And, watched by cockatoos and goats,
Lonely Crusoes building boats;
Where in sunshine reaching out
Eastern cities, miles about,
Are with mosque and minaret
Among sandy gardens set,
And the rich goods from near and far
Hang for sale in the bazaar;
Where the Great Wall round China goes,
And on one side the desert blows,
And with bell and voice and drum,
Cities on the other hum;

Where are forests hot as fire,
Wide as England, tall as a spire,
Full of apes and coconuts
And the lion hunters' huts;
Where the notty crocodile
Lies and blinks in the Nile,
And the red flamingo flies

Hunting fish before his eyes;
Where in jungles near and far,
Man-devouring tigers are,
Lying close and giving ear
Lest the hunt be drawing near,
Or a comer-by be seen
Swinging in a palanquin;
Where among the desert sands
Some deserted city stands.

All its children, sweep and prince,
Grown to manhood ages since,
Not a foot in street or house,
Not a stir of child or mouse,
And when kindly falls the night,
In all the town no spark of light.
There I'll come when I'm a man
With a camel caravan;
Light a fire in the gloom
Of some dusty dining-room;
See the pictures on the walls
Heroes, fights and festivals;
And in a corner find the toys
Of the old Egyptian boys.

MY SHIP AND I

O it's I that am the captain of a tidy little ship,
  Of a ship that goes a-sailing on the pond;
And my ship it keeps a-turning all around and all about;
But when I'm a little older, I shall find the secret out
  How to send my vessel sailing on beyond.

For I mean to grow as little as the dolly at the helm,
  And the dolly I intend to come alive;
And with him beside to help me, it's a-sailing I shall go,
It's a-sailing on the water, when the jolly breezes blow
  And the vessel goes a divie-divie dive.

O it's then you'll see me sailing through the rushes and the reeds,
  And you'll hear the water singing at the prow;
For beside the dolly sailor, I'm to voyage and explore,
To land upon the island where no dolly was before,
  And to fire the penny cannon in the bow.

MY KINGDOM

Down by a shining water well
I found a very little dell,
  No higher than my head.
The heather and the gorse about
In summer bloom were coming out,
  Some yellow and some red.

I called the little pool a sea;
The little hills were big to me;
  For I am very small.
I made a boat, I made a town,
I searched the caverns up and down,
  And named them one and all.

And all about was mine, I said,
The little sparrows overhead,
  The little minnows too.
This was the world and I was king;
For me the bees came by to sing,
  For me the swallows flew.

I played there were no deeper seas,
Nor any wider plains than these,
  No other kings than me.
At last I heard my mother call
Out from the house at even-fall,
  To call me home to tea.

And I must rise and leave my dell,
And leave my dimpled water well,
  And leave my heather blooms.
Alas! and as my home I neared,
How very big my nurse appeared,
  How great and cool the rooms!

THE LITTLE LAND

When at home alone I sit
And am very tired of it,
I have just to shut my eyes
To go sailing through the skies –
To go sailing far away
To the pleasant Land of Play;
To the fairy land afar
Where the Little People are;
Where the clover-tops are trees,
And the rain-pools are the seas,
And the leaves like little ships
Sail about on tiny trips;
And above the daisy tree
  Through the grasses,
High o'erhead the Bumble Bee
  Hums and passes.

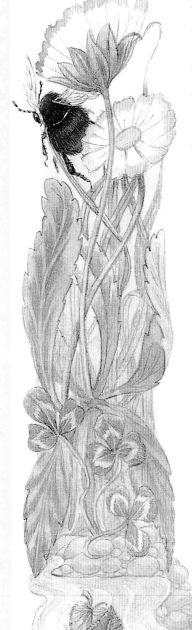

In that forest to and fro
I can wander, I can go;
See the spider and the fly,
And the ants go marching by
Carrying parcels with their feet
Down the green and grassy street.
I can in the sorrel sit,
Where the ladybird alit.
I can climb the jointed grass,
  And on high
See the greater swallows pass
  In the sky,
And the round sun rolling by
Heeding no such things as I.

Through that forest I can pass
Till, as in a looking-glass,
Humming fly and daisy tree
And my tiny self I see,
Painted very clear and neat
On the rain-pool at my feet.
Should a leaflet come to land
Drifting near to where I stand,
Straight I'll board that tiny boat
Round the rain-pool sea to float.

Little thoughtful creatures sit
On the grassy coast of it.
Little things with lovely eyes
See me sailing with surprise.
Some are clad in armour green –
(These have sure to battle been!) –
Some are pied with every hue,
Black and crimson, gold and blue;
Some have wings and swift are gone;
But they all look kindly on.

When my eyes I once again
Open, and see all things plain:
High bare walls, great bare floor;
Great big knobs on drawer and door;
Great big people perched on chairs,
Stitching tucks and mending tears,
Each a hill that I could climb,
And talking nonsense all the time –
  O dear me,
  That I could be
A sailor on the rain-pool sea,
A climber in the clover tree,
And just come back, a sleepy-head,
Late at night to go to bed.

ARMIES IN THE FIRE

The lamps now glitter down the street;
Faintly sound the falling feet;
And the blue even slowly falls
About the garden trees and walls.

Now in the falling of the gloom
The red fire paints the empty room:
And warmly on the roof it looks,
And flickers on the backs of books.

Armies march by tower and spire
Of cities blazing, in the fire;
Till as I gaze with staring eyes,
The armies fade, the lustre dies.

Then once again the glow returns;
Again the phantom city burns;
And down the red-hot valley, lo!
The phantom armies marching go!

Blinking embers, tell me true,
Where are those armies marching to,
And what the burning city is
That crumbles in your furnaces!

PICTURE-BOOKS IN WINTER

Summer fading, winter comes –
Frosty mornings, tingling thumbs,
Window robins, winter rooks,
And the picture story-books.

Water now is turned to stone
Nurse and I can walk upon;
Still we find the flowing brooks
In the picture story-books.

All the pretty things put by,
Wait upon the children's eye,
Sheep and shepherds, trees and crooks,
In the picture story-books.

We may see how all things are,
Seas and cities, near and far,
And the flying fairies' looks,
In the picture story-books.

How am I to sing your praise,
Happy chimney-corner days,
Sitting safe in nursery nooks,
Reading picture story-books?

NIGHT AND DAY

When the golden day is done,
  Through the closing portal,
Child and garden, flower and sun,
  Vanish all things mortal.

As the blinding shadows fall,
  As the rays diminish,
Under evening's cloak, they all
  Roll away and vanish.

Garden darkened, daisy shut,
  Child in bed, they slumber –
Glow-worm in the highway rut,
  Mice among the lumber.

In the darkness houses shine,
  Parents move with candles;
Till, on all, the night divine
  Turns the bedroom handles.

Till at last the day begins
  In the east a-breaking,
In the hedges and the whins
  Sleeping birds a-waking.

In the darkness shapes of things,
  Houses, trees, and hedges,
Clearer grow; and sparrow's wings
  Beat on window ledges.

These shall wake the yawning maid;
  She the door shall open –
Finding dew on garden glade
  And the morning broken.

There my garden grows again
  Green and rosy painted,
As at eve behind the pane
  From my eyes it fainted.

Just as it was shut away,
  Toy-like, in the even,
Here I see it glow with day
  Under glowing heaven.

Every path and every plot,
  Every bush of roses,
Every blue forget-me-not
  Where the dew reposes,

'Up!' they cry, 'the day is come
  On the smiling valleys;
We have beat the morning drum;
  Playmate, join your allies!'

SUMMER SUN

Great is the sun, and wide he goes
Through empty heaven without repose;
And in the blue and glowing days
More thick than rain he showers his rays.

Though closer still the blinds we pull
To keep the shady parlour cool,
Yet he will find a chink or two
To slip his golden fingers through.

The dusty attic, spider-clad,
He, through the keyhole, maketh glad;
And through the broken edge of tiles,
Into the laddered hayloft smiles.

Meantime his golden face around
He bares to all the garden ground,
And sheds a warm and glittering look
Among the ivy's inmost nook.

Above the hills, along the blue,
Round the bright air with footing true,
To please the child, to paint the rose,
The gardener of the World, he goes.

AUTUMN FIRES

In the other gardens
  And all up the vale,
From the autumn bonfires
  See the smoke trail!

Pleasant summer over
  And all the summer flowers,
The red fire blazes,
  The grey smoke towers.

Sing a song of seasons!
  Something bright in all!
Flowers in the summer,
  Fires in the fall!

THE GARDENER

The gardener does not love to talk,
He makes me keep the gravel walk;
And when he puts his tools away,
He locks the door and takes the key.

Away behind the currant row
Where no one else but cook may go,
Far in the plots, I see him dig,
Old and serious, brown and big.

He digs the flowers, green, red, and blue,
Nor wishes to be spoken to.
He digs the flowers and cuts the hay,
And never seems to want to play.

Silly gardener! summer goes,
And winter comes with pinching toes,
When in the garden bare and brown
You must lay your barrow down.

Well now, and while the summer stays,
To profit by these garden days,
O how much wiser you would be
To play at Indian wars with me!

TO AUNTIE

Chief of our aunts – not only I,
But all your dozen of nurslings cry –
What did the other children do?
And what were childhood, wanting you?

NORTH-WEST PASSAGE

1. Good Night

When the bright lamp is carried in,
The sunless hours again begin;
O'er all without, in field and lane,
The haunted night returns again.

Now we behold the embers flee
About the firelit hearth; and see
Our faces painted as we pass,
Like pictures, on the window glass.

Must we to bed indeed! Well then,
Let us arise and go like men,
And face with an udaunted tread
The long black passage up to bed.

Farewell, O brother, sister, sire!
O pleasant party round the fire!
The songs you sing, the tales you tell,
Till far to-morrow, fare ye well!

2. *Shadow March*

All round the house is jet-black night;
  It stares through the window-pane;
It crawls in corners, hiding from the light,
  And it moves with the moving flame.

Now my little heart goes a-beating like a drum,
  With the breath of the Bogie in my hair;
And all round the candle the crooked shadows come
  And go marching up the stair.

The shadow of the balusters, the shadow of the lamp,
  The shadow of the child that goes to bed –
All the wicked shadows coming, tramp, tramp, tramp,
  With the black light overhead.

3. *In Port*

Last, to the chamber where I lie
My fearful footsteps patter nigh,
And come from out the cold and gloom
Into my warm and cheerful room.

There, safe arrived, we turn about
To keep the coming shadows out,
And close the happy door at last
On the perils that we past.

Then, when Mamma goes by to bed,
She shall come in with tip-toe tread,
And see me lying warm and fast
And in the Land of Nod at last.

TO ANY READER

As from the house your mother sees
You playing round the garden trees,
So you may see, if you will look
Through the windows of this book,
Another child, far, far away,
And in another garden, play.
But do not think you can at all,
By knocking on the window, call
That child to hear you. He intent
Is all on his play-business bent.
He does not hear; he will not look,
Nor yet be lured out of his book.
For, long ago, the truth to say,
He has grown up and gone away,
And it is but a child of air
That lingers in the garden there.